12

Hidden Heroes

Bible people who did BRAVE THINGS for God

NT

DayOne

© Day One Publications 2010

First printed 2010

ISBN 978-1-84625-211-2

Published by Day One Publications
Ryelands Road, Leominster, HR6 8NZ

TEL 01568 613 740 FAX 01568 611 473

email—sales@dayone.co.uk

UK web site—www.dayone.co.uk

USA web site—www.dayonebookstore.com

Designed by **documen**

Printed by Thomson Litho, East Kilbride

Dedication

For Ted, Anna and Lydia. I don't know what I would do without you! Thank you for keeping me going and for all your help and ideas.

Contents

Waiting a lifetime
The story of Anna

1

(This story is based on Luke 2:21–40.)

Anna gazed over the sea of faces of those who were waiting to present their children to the priests in the temple. It was a familiar sight. Day after day parents arrived to obey the law that God had given to Moses many years before. Rich and poor, locals and people from far away: all visited the temple forty days after the birth of their babies to thank God for their safe arrival and to ask his blessing on their lives. Over the years Anna had lost count of the number of times she had watched this ceremony, each time with a glimmer of hope in her heart that God would allow her what she longed for.

'Hello, Anna.' A man's voice broke into her thoughts.

Anna turned to see her old friend Simeon standing beside her. 'Simeon?' she said. 'I didn't expect to see you here at the temple today.'

Simeon shook his head. 'God told me to come,' he said quietly. 'And when God speaks, I must do what he says.'

Slowly the old man moved away. Anna followed him with her eyes. Her heart was beating faster than normal. Why had God told Simeon to come here today? Could this be it, the moment they had longed for? She would keep watch!

Anna settled down on one of the seats around the edge of the temple court. She often sat there, watching the world go by, smiling to passers-by and watching the builders continue their work. She had seen so many changes to the temple in her lifetime. When she was young, the temple on this site was an old and crumbling building, but Herod the Great had ordered that it be knocked down and a magnificent new temple be built in its place. There was still a lot of work to do but it was already clear that, when finished, it would be a stunning building.

'Not that a building really matters,' Anna reminded herself quietly. 'It is more important to worship God in your heart.'

'Worship God in your heart'—that was what Anna had sought to do throughout her life. She was now eighty-four years old. She was an old woman, but, although her body might have grown weaker as the years went by, her love for God had grown stronger day by day. Life hadn't worked out for Anna as she had expected. She remembered clearly her wedding day and the first seven happy years of marriage. She had had so many dreams, so many hopes for the future. All that had changed when her husband died. She was so young to be a widow, but, despite her age, she had never remarried and now she lived in the temple, where she could worship God all the time.

Anna's thoughts were brought to a sudden halt. She saw Simeon hurrying towards the temple gate, moving more quickly than she had seen him move for years! He was heading towards a young couple who had just entered the courtyard. They were obviously very poor. They didn't wear fine clothes like some of the people who visited the temple, and Anna had seen the man earlier handing two pigeons to a priest as an offering to God. Two birds was the smallest offering anyone was allowed to bring.

Anna's heart beat even faster. She remembered the words Simeon had repeated to her often over the years: 'Anna, God has told me that I will not die until I have seen the Messiah with my own eyes.'

If other people had told her that God had made them such a promise Anna might not have believed them. After all, the Jewish people had been waiting hundreds of years for God to send his Son, the Messiah, into the world. But Anna knew Simeon so well and totally trusted him to tell the truth. Day after day, year after year, they had watched and waited. They were sure that when the Messiah arrived he would be certain to go to the temple.

Anna watched as Simeon approached the couple. She could see excitement rising on his face. As she watched, the woman gently lifted her baby and laid him in Simeon's arms.

Anna jumped up; this didn't usually happen. Something unusual was definitely going on, and she wasn't going to miss out!

As she approached she could hear Simeon's voice above the murmur of the crowds: 'Lord, you have done what you said. You have let me see the Saviour sent from heaven. Now that you have kept your promise I can die in peace!'

Anna saw the young couple exchange glances. They seemed pleased by what Simeon said, but not totally surprised. It appeared that God had already been speaking to them.

Then Simeon turned to the baby's mother. He spoke gently. 'This child,' he said, 'will change many things in this world. Many will speak out against him and I am afraid that, because of him, you too will be caused much pain.'

The woman nodded. It appeared that this simply confirmed what she already knew.

Anna could not contain herself any longer. She scurried over to them and took the baby in her arms. She was filled with wonder as she looked down into his tiny face. How could it be that this baby would change the world? How could this be God's Son lying peacefully in her arms? There were so many questions, but for now she would just enjoy the moment. She glanced up to look at Simeon. His face was glowing but there were tears in his eyes.

'God kept his promise,' he said softly.

Anna looked back down at the child and nodded. 'As he always does,' she added.

Quietly Anna began to thank God for the precious baby she was cradling. Mary and Joseph, the baby's parents, watched her. They had no idea what lay ahead for them, but they would bring Jesus up as best they could in their small, poor home.

Simeon and Anna stood together as they watched Mary, Joseph and Jesus leave the temple. They would never see them again, but they were happy. They had seen the Saviour of the world!

As soon as they were out of sight Anna hurried back into the temple court and began to talk to people about the baby she had just held. It would be thirty years before anyone else would realize that Jesus really was God's Son sent from heaven, but Anna knew from the start, and her heart was filled with joy.

Anna's name is only mentioned once in the Bible. She is not well known but she is one of the Bible's hidden heroes. She hadn't had an easy life but she didn't sit around allowing herself to be miserable; instead she spent her life worshipping God and praying to him. Sometimes things don't go quite as we would like in our lives. Sometimes we get sick, sometimes people we love die, or other bad things happen to us. Anna shows us that God is always there when things go wrong. The story of Anna also shows us that sometimes our prayers are not answered straight away. Anna and Simeon had waited many years for God to keep his promise to send his Son. They never gave up hope but trusted God to do what he had said.

What do you think?

1. Why do you think Anna lived in the temple?

2. Why do you think God chose to tell two old people that his Son had arrived in the world?

3. Have a look at Luke 2:8–20 to find out which other people knew that the baby Jesus was God's Son.

Bringing others
The story of Andrew

2

*(This story is based on
Mark 1:16–20; 13:3; Luke 5:1–11;
and John 1:35–42; 6:1–15; 12:20–22.)*

Hello, my name is Andrew, and you may not realize this but I was one of the very first people to follow Jesus. I well remember the first time I saw him. I had travelled from my home-town of Bethsaida to listen to the teaching of a man called John the Baptist. John was an unusual sort of person! He wore funny clothes made out of camel's hair and ate locusts and wild honey—not exactly my taste in food! John spent his time travelling near the river Jordan, announcing to people that God was about to keep his promise and send his Son into the world. All the Jewish people had been waiting for hundreds of years for the 'Messiah', as they called him, to arrive. It was so exciting to think that he might be on his way!

Well, I was walking by the river Jordan with John and another friend. John had been telling us that the previous day he had met his cousin Jesus. There wouldn't usually be anything too special about that, except that John told us that this Jesus was actually God's promised Son from heaven, the one everyone had been waiting for! Apparently John had baptized Jesus in the river, and when Jesus came up out of the water, a dove had flown down and landed on him and a loud voice had spoken from heaven. At that moment John knew for certain that at last the Messiah had arrived, although it must have seemed pretty strange that it was his cousin whom he used to play with when they were little!

Anyway, as we walked along, John suddenly stopped and looked straight at a man who was nearby. Then he shouted, 'Look, the Lamb of God!'

We knew immediately what he meant. We walked over to Jesus and began to follow him. He turned round

to us and asked us what we wanted. We simply asked
where he was staying, and he invited us to come and
have a look! We spent the whole day with him. By the
end of the day I knew for certain that what John said
was true. This really was the Messiah; our long wait
was over!

I was so excited! I knew exactly what I wanted to do.
You see, I have a brother called Peter. Peter is quite
different from me. I don't mind being quiet and staying
in the background, but Peter tends to push himself
forward all the time; he likes to be in charge. Well, I just
had to tell him my news; it felt good that I had found out
something before him! I rushed to find him.

'Peter!' I shouted. 'Listen! We have found the Messiah!'

Peter came with me straight away. He wasn't used to
me being the over-excited one, so he was fairly certain that
something unusual was going on! And as soon as Peter
met Jesus I could tell that he felt exactly the same way I
did. We both knew that this man would change our lives
for ever.

After that we didn't see Jesus for a while. Apparently
he went off into the desert, and we carried on our work
as fishermen. We often used to chat about Jesus with our
friends, James and another John, and wondered when we
would see him again.

Then one day we did see him. We were fishing near the
shore of the Sea of Galilee. Peter and I had just cast the net
over the side of the boat when we looked up and saw Jesus
standing on the beach.

'Come, follow me,' he said in a clear voice. 'I will make
you fishers of men.'

That was it! We didn't need any more persuasion. We immediately got out of the boat and followed him. Our lives would never be the same again.

As we walked along the shore with Jesus we saw James and John busily mending their nets. Immediately Jesus asked them to follow him too, and they left their boat with some hired men and joined us. You probably think it's strange that we would leave everything to follow a man we hardly knew, but there was something so different about this man; already God was working in our hearts, making it clear that what he said was true.

After that we four went with Jesus wherever he went. He began to do amazing miracles, like healing the blind and making paralysed men walk. He even did miracles in our own home!

He was staying with us one time when Peter's mother-in-law became very ill. Obviously we told Jesus about it, and he went to her straight away and made her better. News about Jesus's care for an old woman spread rather quickly, and by the evening the whole town seemed to have arrived at our house asking Jesus for healing! Imagine our own home being used by the Son of God!

I remember the following morning well. We thought we had got up early, but Jesus had sneaked out of bed when it was still dark and wasn't in the house. We went to look for him and found him on his own in a quiet place. He had been praying. He always seemed to pray a lot, especially when he was busy. He would often try to stay away from the crowds, sometimes to pray and sometimes to teach us and the other eight men who became his special followers. I loved any time I spent with him.

You know, I may have been the first disciple of Jesus, but it became clear to me quite early on that, if we were to be placed in order of importance, I certainly wouldn't be first! From the start, Peter was seen as the leader; John somehow seemed to be Jesus's closest friend; and James was always included when the other two joined Jesus on special trips. I didn't mind. God has made us all different, and it soon became clear what I was good at: bringing others to Jesus!

I had brought my brother Peter. I had told James and John all about the Messiah. You probably know the amazing story of the feeding of over 5,000 people with five bread rolls and two fish. Well, I was the one who brought the little boy to Jesus. *(You can read the little boy's story in the next chapter.)* I knew that Jesus could do something wonderful with any little gift that we brought to him.

Another thing I realized about Jesus was that he had time for anyone. I remember the way little children used to come to him and he never turned them away. I remember how he had time for people whom no one else loved, and for people who came from other countries. I remember when some Greeks came to ask us if they could talk to Jesus. I took them to him straight away; I knew that he would always have time for strangers.

It was awful when Jesus was arrested and killed. I had been with him in the garden when the soldiers came. Like a coward, I ran away with the other disciples; I wish I hadn't. Still, he forgave us when he came back to life again! What a day that was! There was no doubt any more: Jesus was God's promised Messiah, and we had been given the greatest privilege in the world!

The last time I saw Jesus was on the Mount of Olives just outside Jerusalem. He asked us to go throughout the world telling everyone about him. Then, as we watched, he went back up into heaven and a cloud hid him from our sight. An angel appeared and promised us that one day Jesus would come back again. We all felt so scared and unhappy, but Jesus sent us a gift from heaven: the Holy Spirit. When he filled our lives we weren't frightened any more, but we did what he had asked and travelled all over the place, telling people about him.

So my story isn't a hero's story. I was never very well known as a disciple; in fact, there is very little recorded about me in the Bible. That doesn't matter. What matters is that I brought people to Jesus and I followed him all the days of my life.

Andrew is one of the least-known disciples of Jesus. He is one of the Bible's hidden heroes. He was willing to stay in the background and simply introduce others to Jesus. Andrew is a great example to us. There are not many people who become famous in their lives, but that doesn't matter to God. What God wants is that we use the gifts he has given us to the best of our ability. He also wants us to tell our friends about Jesus and to live our lives in a way that points others to him.

What do you think?

1. Why do you think that Andrew rushed to tell his brother that he had met Jesus?

2. In the Bible it tells us that people take notice of what others are like on the outside, but God looks at our hearts (see 1 Samuel 16:7). Why is this important in the story of Andrew?

3. Do you think God prefers people who are outgoing, like Peter, or quiet, like Andrew? Psalm 139:13–14 may give you a clue!

Take it all!

The story of the boy who gave up his lunch

3

*(This story is based on
John chapter 6, Luke chapter 9,
Mark chapter 6 and Matthew chapter 14.
The Bible doesn't tell us the name of the
boy in this story, but we are going to call
him Joshua. Some of this story is exactly
as the Bible tells it. Other parts are what
the author imagines may have happened.)*

Joshua was excited. He had heard so many stories about this man called Jesus who could apparently do all sorts of amazing miracles. His father had told him that Jesus could make blind people see and deaf people hear! He had even heard that Jesus had brought a boy from the town of Nain back to life after he had died! Now, at last, he might get to see him!

Joshua had begged his mum for weeks to be allowed to go and see Jesus if he ever came to a town near them. And now it had happened! Joshua could hardly believe it. Imagine! The famous Jesus was actually there, only a short way from his home in the small fishing village of Bethsaida. Joshua jigged up and down in excitement.

'Joshua,' his mum scolded, 'calm down! You can't go until I've made your lunch and I can't make the bread cook any quicker. You will have to wait.'

Joshua hopped from one foot to the other. Why did time always drag so slowly when something exciting was happening?

At last, his mother lifted the steaming bread rolls from the oven and packed them into a leather bag, alongside some other food.

'Now,' she said firmly, 'you be good. Watch out for chariots and don't get into trouble.'

'Yes, Mum,' shouted Joshua, running for the door. 'I promise.'

Joshua was a healthy boy, and it wasn't long before he had run the mile or so to the remote ground further along the shore-line of the Sea of Galilee. He often played there with his friends, but it looked different now! Joshua stopped and stared. There must have been over five thousand people spread out all over the hillside: young and old, men and women, and children playing and laughing in the sunshine. A few people waved as Joshua walked towards them.

'So you heard that Jesus is coming too,' laughed one man, as Joshua approached. 'Looks like you didn't expect there to be so many people.'

Joshua shrugged his shoulders. He felt disappointed. He had hoped there would be just a few people so he could get close to Jesus, maybe even speak to him. Now he was stuck at the back of a huge crowd.

Suddenly, everyone fell silent. All eyes were fixed on a man who was standing at the front of the crowd.

'That's him,' whispered someone nearby. 'That's Jesus!'

Joshua craned his neck to see more clearly. If that was Jesus, he didn't look at all as he had expected. He just looked like an ordinary man. You would have walked past him in the street without taking the tiniest bit of notice. Then Jesus began to speak …

The sun was dropping in the sky when Jesus stopped speaking and began to talk to some of his friends at the front of the crowd. Joshua glanced around. Everyone seemed to feel the same. They had listened to Jesus for hours but no one had noticed the time, they had been so caught up in every word of his teaching. Joshua had never heard anything like it before and now he was more determined than ever to meet the man.

Gently he eased his way through the crowds, listening as he went.

'Can you believe we've been here so long?'

'I've never heard anyone teach like he does. Are you sure he's only a carpenter's son?'

One comment in particular stood out to Joshua above all the others. It was made by a small boy as he tugged at his mother's coat.

'Mum, I'm starving!'

It was then that Joshua realized how hungry he was. He hadn't eaten since breakfast. Longingly, he felt the shape of the bread rolls in his bag. He was desperate to eat them but, if he was going to try to get near to Jesus, now was definitely the time to do it, while people were busy talking. He continued forwards.

Reaching the front of the crowd, Joshua tried to ease himself slowly closer to Jesus. He could hear him talking to his friends; they were discussing food.

'Lord,' said one of them, 'you'll have to send all these people away to eat. Some of them have been here all day and they must be so hungry.'

'You feed them then, Philip,' Jesus replied.

Philip looked around at his friends. They all smirked and shrugged their shoulders.

'Lord, we haven't got any food,' said someone else. 'Even if there were shops near here, it would take more than eight months' wages to feed them all!'

Philip laughed. 'And even if we had that much money, there would only be enough for everyone to have one bite,' he said, shaking his head.

Jesus looked at them and quietly spoke again: 'You feed them.'

It was then that an idea sprang into Joshua's head, and, no matter how hard he tried to push it out again, it just wouldn't go away. It was a silly idea. What use could it possibly be? There were just too many people. But the idea wouldn't go away, so slowly Joshua left the safety of the crowd and walked towards Jesus. He tugged on the sleeve of a man he had heard was called Andrew.

'Excuse me,' he said in his politest voice, 'I thought Jesus might be hungry. He can have my dinner if he wants it. There's not that much.'

Andrew looked down at the five rolls and the two fish lying in Joshua's grubby hands and smiled.

'Lord,' he said leading Joshua right up to Jesus, 'there's a boy here who says you can have his lunch. He's got five loaves and two fish. That won't go far with all these people.'

Joshua watched Jesus carefully. His dad had told him that Jesus liked children and never turned them away. Now, as he looked into Jesus's eyes, he knew that he had done the right thing.

'Ask everyone to sit down in groups of about fifty,' Jesus told his friends.

A silence descended on the whole crowd again as they were instructed to sit on the grass. Every eye was focused on Jesus. There was excitement in the air.

Jesus held Joshua's dinner in his hands, looked up to heaven and gave thanks to God. Then he ordered his friends to hand round the food.

Joshua watched in amazement. This wasn't some kind of magic trick. It couldn't be! It was his dinner, but somehow it was being handed round from person to person, group after group, and there was still plenty. How could this be happening?

Jesus saw Joshua's face and spoke to him. 'You don't understand what has happened, do you?'

Joshua shook his head.

'There are many things in life that you won't understand,' Jesus continued, 'but always remember this. With God, nothing is impossible. He can take what little you have and use it in an amazing way.'

As darkness began to fall, Joshua wandered back home to his mother. He had been so excited when he had set off that morning, and he had not been disappointed. No, he didn't understand everything, but he had seen amazing things, and he knew his life was changed for ever.

Sometimes, when we hear Bible stories about amazing people doing fantastic things, we can feel that there is nothing much that we can do for Jesus. The miracle that Jesus performed when he fed five thousand people is very famous, but it's good to remember that he used a kind little boy who was willing to share his lunch. This boy is one of the Bible's hidden heroes. He is not well known, but his small actions helped to change people's lives. Today, God can use the little things that we can do to make a huge difference to those around us.

What do you think?

1. How do you think the boy felt when Andrew took him to Jesus to show him the five loaves and two fish?

2. Read what it says in Matthew 19:13–15. Why does this show us that the boy didn't need to be scared when he approached Jesus?

3. What does the story of the feeding of the five thousand teach us about Jesus?

4. What does this story teach us about our attitude to the things that we have?

Two small coins

The story of the widow's gift

4

(This story is based on Luke 21:1–4 and Mark 12:41–44. The Bible doesn't tell us the name of the lady in this story but we are going to call her Sara. Some of this story is exactly as the Bible tells it. Other parts are what the author imagines may have happened.)

Sara hurried through the crowded streets of Jerusalem towards the temple. She could see it in the distance, standing tall above the rest of the city, its stonework still bright and new. It was a magnificent building! Herod the Great had made lots of mistakes during his reign as king, but he had certainly done a good job with the construction of the temple. It had been forty-six years since he had ordered that a new temple be built and, although there was still work to be done on the outer buildings, the main inner courts were now complete. Somehow its huge size and beautiful gold trimmings, glimmering in the sunlight, emphasized the greatness of the God who was worshipped there.

Sara loved to go to the temple. For her, it wasn't just a place of worship but also somewhere she could go simply to be around people. It had been a lonely life since her husband had died. She missed him greatly, and often wished she had someone she could go home to and chatter to about all the little things that had happened during each day. She wished he could have been at the temple with her a few days ago; he would have enjoyed that!

That day, Jerusalem had been packed full of visitors. Many of them had lined the streets cheering as Jesus entered the city. People had placed their coats on the ground or pulled leaves off trees for the donkey carrying Jesus to walk on. Everyone seemed delighted to see him. He had gone up to the temple and looked at everything going on there, but it was getting dark and he had left quickly with his friends. The next day he was back!

As Jesus had walked into the temple it had been obvious that something was going to happen. He marched immediately over to the men selling cattle and sheep and began to drive all the animals out of the courtyard. He grabbed hold of the tables full of doves and turned them upside down, and swiped all the money off the money-changers' tables. Sara smiled as she remembered the shocked looks on everyone's face! She knew her husband would have been glad. The men selling the animals for sacrifice always charged far too much, and the money-changers always demanded enormous amounts to change ordinary money into coins accepted in the temple. Sara had agreed with the words that Jesus had shouted: 'This should be a place of prayer,' he had bellowed, 'but you have turned it into a den of robbers!'

Now Sara was arriving at the temple. It seemed quieter than usual; she thought she knew what that meant! As expected, there were fewer sellers in the temple court, but Jesus was there, speaking to the large crowds that had gathered. Sara positioned herself carefully, close enough to hear every word that Jesus was saying, but far enough away to draw no attention to herself.

Many in the crowd were asking Jesus questions. It was obvious that many of them were trying to get Jesus to say something that they could complain about. However, Jesus seemed to answer each question without any difficulty.

Sara loved to listen to him. He made her feel important. So many of the religious leaders looked down their noses at widows like her. They seemed to think she was worthless; after all, she had no money to give to the temple. Quietly

Sara jingled the two coins in her pocket. This was all she had left in the world. What she was going to do with it would have seemed like foolishness to some people, but she was certain that this was what she wanted. She might be poor but she still trusted in God, and, if what Jesus said was true, it didn't matter to God if you were rich or poor. What mattered was how much you loved him.

Slowly she walked across the temple courtyard. There were so many people around! She stopped for a moment and watched them all—the priests in their fine, flowing robes, the religious leaders praying in loud voices. She wondered what God would think about them.

Looking up, she realized with horror that Jesus was now sitting with his friends close to the place towards which she was heading. He seemed to be watching with interest what was going on. Person after person was walking towards the treasury box to put in some money as an offering to God. All the rich people seemed to throw their money into the box with such a clatter. Some of them lifted their money bags high to pour in the coins so that everyone could see how much they were giving. For a moment, Sara felt silly. What was the point of her giving two tiny copper coins? They were worth so little. What if someone saw her?

She sidled slowly towards the box, her hands clammy around the tiny coins. She waited until she was sure that no one was looking and then pulled her hand out of her pocket and placed it deep into the treasury box, hoping that nobody would see the tiny amount she was giving. Then she quickly walked away.

It was as she passed Jesus that she realized someone had seen.

'I tell you the truth,' she heard Jesus say gently to his friends, 'this poor widow gave more than everyone else. She gave everything she had.'

Looking up, Sara saw Jesus looking at her. Suddenly her heart felt full of joy. What she believed about Jesus really was true! It didn't matter to him how much money she had. He could see what was going on inside her. He knew that she was poor, but he also knew that she loved God very much, and that was far more important to him.

The lady in this story would have had no idea that over 2,000 years later millions of people all over the world would have heard about her. She was very poor and must have felt that she had nothing much to give. However, Jesus turned her into one of the Bible's hidden heroes. This lady gave what she had and, even though that was a tiny amount, it was enough for Jesus, because it was given out of a heart that wanted God to have everything. As children we may feel that we have nothing important to give to Jesus. We must remember that Jesus sees us on the inside and that what he wants most is that our hearts are full of love for him.

What do you think?

1. Some visitors to the temple gave huge amounts of
    money, so why does Jesus say that Sara gave more than
    anyone else?

2. The Bible tells us that Jesus was angry when he turned
    over the tables of the money-changers. Sometimes it's
    hard to imagine that Jesus had the same feelings that
    we have. Have a look at the following verses to see
    what other feelings Jesus had:

    ~ John 11:35

    ~ John 4:6

    ~ Matthew 4:2

    ~ Matthew 26:38.

Bravery at dusk

The story of Joseph of Arimathea

5

*(This story is based on
Matthew 27:57–61; Mark 15:43–46;
Luke 23:50–55; and John 19:38–42.)*

Quietly Joseph shut the door of his house and leaned his aching head against the cold stone wall. He had never meant it to end like this. He should have spoken out more strongly. Maybe he could have stopped them. Why was he such a coward?

Wearily he slumped into a chair and closed his eyes. It was no use. All he could see was Jesus, and that was the picture he wanted desperately to push out of his mind.

He was so tired. He had been up most of the night as Jesus was passed from one group of people to another in the hope that someone would make the decision as to what to do with him. Eventually, the sun had come up and the vote had been cast. Jesus would be killed. At least he had voted against that decision. He was glad that his friend Nicodemus had protested against the decision too.

Once the decision was made, everything had happened so quickly. Jesus was taken outside the city and crucified. Thankfully he had died more quickly than expected. Joseph winced; it had still taken three hours! He had stood at a distance and watched.

Joseph stood up and began to pace up and down the room. The problem was that Jesus's body was still on the cross, and Joseph couldn't bear the thought of that! After all, Jesus had done nothing wrong. Yes, he had claimed to be God's Son sent from heaven, but surely all the miracles he had done showed that what he said was true ... and now he was dead!

Suddenly Joseph came to a decision. He was a well-respected man with an important position on the Jewish Council. He even knew Pilate, the Roman leader in Jerusalem. It was too late to save Jesus's life, but he could at least give him a decent burial. He hurried outside. His mind was spinning. He couldn't do this alone, but he was sure that his friend Nicodemus would help him. He would call in at his home on the way to the palace.

'Sir,' announced a servant to Pilate. 'Joseph from the Jewish Council is here. He is asking to see you.'

'Send him in,' ordered Pilate.

With great fear Joseph entered the grand surroundings of the Roman palace.

'I'm sorry to disturb you,' he said bravely, 'but I've come to ask your permission to remove Jesus's body from the cross and to place him in a tomb.'

Pilate looked confused. 'Surely he can't be dead already?' he said.

Joseph nodded. 'He is, sir,' he replied.

Pilate sent immediately for the Roman soldier who had been on duty at the foot of Jesus's cross.

'This man says that Jesus has already died,' Pilate said. 'Is this true?'

'Absolutely true,' the centurion confirmed. 'I was on duty the whole time and I watched him die. There is no chance at all that he is still living.'

Pilate didn't need time to think. He too had been awake all night, trying to decide whether he should allow Jesus to be killed. Even his wife had sent him a message saying that he must have no part in the death of Jesus because he was a totally innocent man. In the end Pilate had been too weak and afraid to do what he believed to be right. He had washed his hands in front of all the people to show that he didn't agree with killing Jesus, yet he had still let the crucifixion go ahead. Somehow he thought it might make him feel a little better if Jesus was at least laid in a tomb.

'You can take the body,' he said. 'Do what you like with it.'

Gratefully Joseph left the palace and headed along the path towards the place where Jesus had been crucified. Suddenly he heard a whispered voice.

'Joseph!'

Startled, he turned around.

'Nicodemus!' he exclaimed. 'You've come.'

Nicodemus nodded. 'When you said you were going to see Pilate, I knew I had to help you,' he said quietly. 'You're so much braver than me. Even when Jesus was alive I only dared visit him when it was dark, just in case anyone saw me.'

'We've both kept it a secret that we followed Jesus,' said Joseph sadly. 'Maybe we shouldn't have been so scared of the other Council members, but what is done is done. Now at least we have a chance to do something for him.'

Nicodemus nodded. 'Come on,' he said. 'We need to be quick. It's going to be dark soon. Where are we going to put the body?'

'In my tomb,' answered Joseph. 'It's only just been made in the garden. It's clean and new, and it's not too far to carry him.'

So the two men hurried up the hill. Once there, they carefully lifted Jesus's body down off the cross and laid it gently on the ground.

'I've brought some special spices,' whispered Nicodemus.

'And I've brought strips of cloth,' added Joseph. 'So at least we can give him the type of burial that Jewish men should have.'

Together, in silence, the two men wrapped Jesus's body. It seemed so wrong. He was innocent. He didn't deserve this.

With great sorrow they carried the body into the nearby garden and laid it carefully in Joseph's tomb, which was cut out of the rock face. Darkness was falling quickly now. Hurriedly the two men left Jesus in the tomb and went outside. Together they pushed the huge stone into place in front of the tomb entrance, the loud grating noise echoing round the garden as the stone slipped into the channel that ensured it stayed in place.

'He's safe in there,' whispered Nicodemus. 'No one could move that stone!'

They slowly turned to leave, but jumped violently as they saw two women standing opposite the tomb and watching them closely. Joseph recognized them immediately, although he knew little about them. He knew they were both called Mary and that he had often seen them listening to Jesus. He also knew that he had seen them standing near the cross. Now it seemed they had kept watch, following him and Nicodemus to see where the body of their precious friend was placed. He was sure they would be back, but they would have to wait two days before they could add their own spices to the body. It was nearly Saturday, and no Jewish person was allowed to do any sort of work on the day they called 'the Sabbath'.

Joseph and Nicodemus sadly wandered from the garden and made their way along the path.

'Surely this can't be the end,' muttered Nicodemus, breaking the silence.

Joseph shook his head. 'We weren't brave enough to tell everyone that we thought Jesus was the Messiah,' he whispered. 'But I really did believe it. I just wish I'd told him I followed him while he was still alive.'

Nicodemus gently took hold of his friend's shoulder. 'When he was alive he taught a lot about forgiveness,' he said softly. 'And at least in the end you were brave enough to show that you loved him. Goodnight, Joseph.'

Joseph smiled weakly as he took the path towards his home. Nicodemus's words brought some comfort. He was so glad he had been brave enough to visit Pilate. Maybe he had been a secret follower in the past, but soon everyone would know what he had done that night. Somehow Joseph didn't mind any more.

This would be rather a sad story if Jesus had stayed in Joseph's tomb for ever. However, the story has a brilliant ending. The two Marys did go back to the tomb on the Sunday, but when they arrived the stone had been rolled away and the tomb was empty! Jesus was alive again! After that, many people saw Jesus. The Bible doesn't tell us if he met up with Joseph, but it seems pretty likely that both Joseph and Nicodemus would have seen him. That must have been amazing!

For much of his life Joseph didn't openly follow Jesus. It may be strange to think that he is one of the Bible's hidden heroes. However, Joseph realized that he had been wrong and bravely tried to make up for the mistakes he had made. In the end, he acted out of love for Jesus and a deep desire to do the right thing. All of us will make many mistakes in our lives. We need to remember that, like Joseph, it is never too late to put things right and to have the courage to follow Jesus.

What do you think?

1. Why do you think Joseph wanted to show his love for Jesus in this way?

2. Why do you think that Joseph and Nicodemus were such good friends?

3. This could be rather a sad story if we didn't know that it had a happy ending! Have a look at Luke 24:5–6 to see what happened!

An unexpected voice!

The story of Ananias

6

*(This story is based on
Acts 9:1–22 and 22:10–16.)*

Ananias walked back to his house with a heavy heart. He and his friends would not be meeting again for a while; it was safer to wait until the danger had passed. Those meetings were usually times of great joy as they prayed and worshipped God together, but tonight everyone had been subdued. A message had arrived from the Christians in Jerusalem, warning them that Saul was on his way to Damascus with a group of soldiers. His aim was to arrest anyone he found who was a follower of Jesus and take them back to prison.

Ananias and his friends had heard so much about Saul. Already, in Jerusalem, he had placed many Christians in prison and arranged for many others to be killed. Now he was on his way to do the same thing in Damascus, and apparently he would arrive tomorrow! It was better to stay in hiding for a few weeks until he had returned home.

That night, Ananias got little sleep. Thoughts of Saul flashed through his mind. Would Saul arrest him? Which of his friends would be taken to Jerusalem? Surely not everyone could remain hidden; Saul had ways of making people talk!

The next morning, he couldn't concentrate on anything. He strained his ears for the noise of the soldiers' arrival; even the smallest noise seemed to make him jump. Surely Saul must have arrived by now!

Suddenly, he stopped what he was doing. He felt cross with himself. Why was he worrying? When Jesus was on earth, he had taught that there was no need to worry about anything, as he would always be there with his people.

He bowed his head. 'Lord,' he prayed, 'we are all so frightened, but we ask you to keep us safe and to help us trust you for whatever happens.'

Immediately Ananias felt at peace. The problem of Saul was still there, but he knew that God was right there with him.

But what was that?

Ananias was sure he had heard a voice. He looked around. There was no one there!

'Ananias!'

Suddenly Ananias realized that God was speaking directly to him.

'Yes, Lord?' he answered in a whisper.

'Ananias, I want you to go to Straight Street, to the house of Judas. Saul is there already. He has gone blind. I have told him that a man called Ananias will come to see him to restore his sight.'

Ananias was stunned.

'But Lord,' he said, 'I've heard so many stories about Saul. I know he's come here to Damascus to arrest anyone who follows you.'

'Ananias, I want you to go,' God replied. 'I have chosen Saul to go and tell many people the truth about me. In future, it will be Saul who will suffer for following me.'

Immediately Ananias got up to do what God said. As he approached Straight Street, he was both excited and scared. It seemed that God was about to do something fantastic and he, Ananias, was about to be part of it! But, at the same time, he was about to walk into the house of the man who had harmed so many other Christians.

Judas opened the door and pointed to where Saul was sitting. As soon as Ananias saw him, he placed his hands on Saul's head and prayed.

'Saul,' he said, 'the Lord Jesus, who appeared to you as you approached Damascus, has sent me here so that you may be able to see again.'

Immediately it was as if scales fell from Saul's eyes and he could see!

Then Ananias continued, 'Saul, God has chosen you to take the message of Jesus to many people. You must ask God for his forgiveness and be baptized.'

Straight away, Saul did what Ananias told him. His life was changed!

Over a meal, Saul explained to Ananias exactly what had happened earlier that day. He and the soldiers had been approaching Damascus. It was almost midday. Suddenly, there was a bright light from heaven. He had fallen to the ground and a voice had spoken to him.

'Saul, Saul, why are you persecuting me?'

'Who are you, Lord?' Saul had asked.

'I am Jesus,' said the voice. 'Get up! Go to Damascus, and I will show you what to do.'

So Saul had done as Jesus said. He was directed to the house of Judas and he waited. Ananias told Saul the rest of the story. It was hard to believe! That morning, Saul had been ready to destroy the Christians, and Ananias had been terrified. Now they sat together eating, both of them followers of Jesus. They both smiled. God could certainly do surprising things!

Over the next few days, Ananias introduced Saul to many of his friends. At first, they were all suspicious.

Wasn't this the same man who had come to Damascus
to arrest them? Had Ananias gone mad? Was Saul just
pretending that he was a follower of Jesus so that he could
bring the Christians out of hiding? Would he then turn on
them and arrest them all? But as soon as they met Saul,
their fears disappeared. He was definitely a changed man.
He seemed to want to talk about Jesus all the time, and he
even went into the Jewish temples preaching.

From then on, Saul spent the rest of his life telling
others about Jesus. He was beaten, stoned, shipwrecked
and hated, and he faced many other dangerous situations.
He spent the later part of his life in prison. Even then, Saul
didn't stop speaking about Jesus. From there, he wrote
many of the books that are included in our Bible today!

Saul became one of the most famous people in the Bible.
His name was later changed to Paul. We don't know what
happened to Ananias, but we do know that Ananias is
one of the Bible's hidden heroes. He was willing to do
what God asked him to do, even though it seemed strange
and dangerous. He knew God well enough to recognize
his voice, and he trusted God to keep him safe. He is a
great example to us! Ananias was also willing to give
Saul a chance to change, despite the harm that he had
done to so many of Ananias's friends. This story shows
us how important it is to always be willing to forgive and
give someone a second chance. It also teaches us that
the power and love of God can change even the worst of
people. Ananias obeyed God and went to see Saul, but

he went beyond that, looking for ways to help Saul fit
into the church. If Ananias hadn't introduced Saul to the
Christians in Damascus, it is unlikely that Saul would have
been welcomed in the way that he was. We need to follow
Ananias's example.

What do you think?

1. How do you think Ananias must have felt as he
    knocked on the door of Judas's house?

2. Many people became followers of Jesus through
    hearing the disciples talk about him. Why do you think
    God appeared personally to Saul and spoke to him
    so clearly?

3. How do you think Ananias felt as he went home that
    evening after meeting Saul?

Busy sewing
The story of Dorcas

7

(This story is based on Acts 9:32–43.)

Peter hurried along the road from Lydda to Joppa.
He could tell that the two young men with him were
growing impatient, but he was going as quickly as he could!
The speed at which they were walking gave him little time
to think, but, between breaths, a question kept niggling
away at the back of his mind: Why would two young men
walk (or rather run) for twelve miles to fetch him, Peter,
just because one lady had died?

Peter knew that life was valuable, especially for close
family and friends, but people died all the time and
normally there wasn't too much fuss about it. Yet these
two men had heard that he was in Joppa and had come
immediately to beg him to go with them to the house of
someone he had never met called Dorcas. Apparently she
had died, and they hoped that he could help! Peter had seen
the desperation on the men's faces and had gone with them
immediately. He knew the only hope was that God would
bring her back to life.

Peter could hear the wailing as soon as he arrived
in Joppa. Quickly the young men led him along the
street towards Dorcas's house, where crowds of people
were standing outside, crying. Looking around, Peter
was surprised by the mixture of people there; it seemed
that Dorcas was well-thought-of by rich and poor alike.
However, as he glanced at the wailing, tear-stained faces
of the women and children, he realized that this was
more than a normal show of sadness. There was a look of
great loss on every face in the crowd, as if something very
precious had been taken from them. Peter wondered what
sort of woman Dorcas had been. Her house didn't stand
out as anything special compared with the others along the

street, and he felt sure that he would have known if her
family was particularly famous. Why was it that so many
people had turned up to mourn her death?

The men ushered Peter inside the house and led him up
the stairs to the room where Dorcas had been laid carefully
on a bed. The room was packed with women, and all of
them seemed to want to talk to Peter at once.

'Look at this that I'm wearing,' said one lady, pointing
to a beautifully made robe. 'Dorcas made this for me. I've
had no money since my husband died a few years ago and
I was often cold—but I'm not any more, thanks to Dorcas.'

'Look at my children here,' interrupted another voice.
Peter turned to see a young lady with three small children
by her side. 'Dorcas made all our clothes. My husband is
dead too. No one really cares for us, apart from Dorc—'
She broke off, unable to speak as tears poured down
her face.

'Everything I'm wearing was made by Dorcas,' joined
in another lady. 'She charged me no money. She had great
love in her heart. She said that love came from God.'

An older lady approached Peter. She spoke quietly,
sadness etched on her face. 'There was no one else like her,'
she whispered. 'She was always doing good and helping the
poor. It didn't matter who they were, Dorcas would care for
them. She made clothes for all the widows in this room and
many more who are outside. She always did anything she
could to help even the poorest, most undeserving person. It
is the saddest day we can imagine. Our lives will never be
the same if she is not here.'

Peter looked again around the room and shook his head.
He could hardly believe that one woman could have had

such a huge effect on so many lives. There was no time
to lose!

'Everyone please leave the room!' he ordered in a
loud voice.

Slightly shocked, all the women obeyed and trooped out
of the door. As soon as he was alone Peter got down on his
knees and began to pray. He believed in the power of God.
Ever since Jesus had gone back to heaven God had used
Peter and the other disciples to perform many wonderful
miracles, but so far none of them had raised someone from
the dead. This was new to Peter, but he had seen Jesus
bring people back to life and, although Jesus was no longer
with them, he knew that God's power hadn't changed.

Believing that God was about to do something amazing,
Peter rose to his feet and walked over to the bed.

He gazed down at Dorcas's white face and spoke clearly
to her: 'Dorcas, get up!'

Immediately, Dorcas sat up and looked around the
familiar room! Peter smiled at her, took her gently by the
hand and helped her to her feet.

'Hello, Dorcas,' he said softly. 'I'm Peter. There are
many people waiting to see you. It seems that God still has
a lot that he wants you to do with your life.'

'You can come in now,' he called to the women on
the other side of the door. 'Come and see that God can
do anything!'

The women ran into the room and gazed open-mouthed
at Dorcas. In great excitement, one of them ran to the
window and threw it open. 'All of you come and look
at this!' she shouted to those gathered outside. 'Dorcas
is alive!'

People began to push their way through the crowds to see for themselves whether what they had heard was true. Arriving in the upstairs room, each of them saw Dorcas standing there chatting to her friends. She really was alive and well!

The news that Dorcas had been raised from the dead spread quickly from person to person. Over the next few days, more and more people visited Dorcas's home to see whether she really was alive. Having seen God do such an amazing miracle, many of them became followers of Jesus too.

Peter stayed in Joppa for a while at the house of a man called Simon. He wanted time to teach all the new followers more about Jesus, but he also wanted to get to know this special lady who had been used by God to change so many people's lives.

The Bible doesn't tell us anything else about Dorcas. As Peter stayed in Joppa for a while it seems likely that she spent time with him, getting to know him and being taught by him. No doubt as soon as she had been raised from the dead she continued to sew clothes for the widows and their children and help the poor. Dorcas was never rich or famous. We know very little about her, but what we do know shows us that she was one of the Bible's hidden heroes. She was a woman whose heart was full of love for those around her. She recognized that God doesn't care only for rich and successful people, but also for the poor who have nothing. She used her gift of sewing to make beautiful clothes for the poor, and she spent her whole life doing good to those around her. The story of Dorcas teaches us how important God thinks it is that we try to do good to others and to help the poor. Most of us have lovely homes and nice clothes to wear. We need to remember that God has given these to us, and always be willing to share what we have with other people.

What do you think?

1. Have a look at James 2:26. How does this verse relate to the story of Dorcas?

2. Why do you think Dorcas spent so much time and money helping the poor?

3. Who do you think was more important— Peter or Dorcas?

By the river
The story of Lydia

8

*(This story is based on
Acts 16:6–40 and 20:1–6.)*

L ydia could hardly contain her excitement. It had been almost four years since their first meeting outside the city gates of Philippi. Today they would meet again, down by the river. Lydia often went to this meeting place with her friends, but today she was walking alone. She was glad. She was often so busy with her business that she got little time to herself, and to have a few moments with nothing but her thoughts felt special. As she walked, Lydia played over in her mind the events of the first day they had met. The time had passed so quickly since then. So much had happened. So many lives had changed, including her own.

It had been the Sabbath, the special day when Jewish people would stop work, as God said they should, to have a rest and take time to worship him. Lydia was not a Jew but, over the years, she had come to believe in God, and often on the Sabbath she would gather with friends down by the river to pray. Usually there would just be a group of women there. They would catch up on all the news from the city and then pray together for a while before returning to their homes. However, this particular Sabbath was to be different.

The women had only just arrived at the river when they heard the sound of men's voices floating through the air.

'Sometimes I'm glad when there's no building for worship in a city,' they heard one voice say.

'Me too,' replied another. 'There's something special about being out in the open air, looking at the beauty of the world while you worship the God who made it all.'

The men had seemed surprised when they walked round the corner and found the group of women sitting on the rocks. They had obviously been looking for somewhere quiet, and they weren't going to find it here!

Lydia remembered how cross she had felt when she first saw them. All through the week she ran a successful business selling purple cloth to rich people and she didn't get much free time. The afternoon of the Sabbath was the only chance she had to relax and meet up with her friends. As soon as the men had started to speak, however, she had been fascinated by what they said. It was the one called Paul who did most of the talking. He told them about a man called Jesus who had apparently changed his life!

As she listened, Lydia was certain that he was telling the truth. Suddenly she understood. God had sent his Son, Jesus, into the world. Jesus had died to take the punishment that she deserved for all the wrong things that she had done in her life. The great news was that Jesus wasn't dead any more! He had come back to life and had then returned to his Father in heaven. If she asked him to, he would forgive her at any time and then, even though he was now in heaven, would stay by her side for the rest of her life! Lydia knew straight away that this was what she wanted more than anything in the world.

In great excitement Lydia had hurried back to her home and told her family and servants that they must go with her to the river. When they arrived Paul and his friends explained the truth about Jesus to all of them, and the whole family had believed what they said. Immediately they were all baptized in the river to make it clear to everyone in Philippi that, from now on, they were followers of Jesus.

From that moment, Lydia's life changed. She straight away persuaded Paul and his friends to stay at her home, and soon lots of people began to join them day after day so that they too could hear the message about Jesus.

As she walked along, Lydia chortled to herself. Having Paul around certainly added a bit of excitement to her life! They hadn't been in her home long before Paul and his friend Silas got into trouble for healing somebody's slave-girl. The girl's owners were furious as they had made lots of money out of her in the past. They stirred up trouble, and Paul and Silas had been thrown into prison.

Lydia had been shocked that her visitors were in jail but she knew that they had done nothing wrong. Quickly she invited anyone who believed in Jesus round to her house. Together they prayed that God would do something amazing and that somehow Paul and Silas would be released. They had prayed all night. Then, just after it had become light, there had been a knock at the door. Lydia had rushed to answer it, and standing outside were Paul and Silas!

What a story they had to tell! They had been beaten and then chained to a wall in the darkness, with their feet in stocks. Despite being uncomfortable they were determined not to be miserable and began to sing songs and to pray. All the other prisoners had been listening to them when, without warning, the ground began to shake.

'It's an earthquake!' screamed one of the prisoners.

As he shouted, all the prison doors flew open and the chains of all the prisoners fell off. It was hard to see what was happening in the darkness, but suddenly the dark cells were lit up by the bright lamp of the jailer as he rushed to see what was going on. When he saw that the prison doors were all wide open and the prisoners were no longer

chained up, he was terrified and pulled out his sword.
Immediately Paul shouted to him not to be afraid because
all the prisoners were safe and none had escaped. Straight
away the jailer realized there was something special about
these two men. He ran over to Paul and Silas, fell down on
his knees before them, and asked them what he could do to
be saved. As Paul began to explain to him all about Jesus,
the jailer sent a message to his family and his servants,
telling them to come and listen to what Paul had to say.
Right there in the middle of the night, all the jailer's
family became followers of Jesus. The jailer took Paul and
Silas into his home. He washed their wounds, gave them
food and new clothes, and then he and all his family were
baptized. It had been such a happy time!

As soon as they were let out of prison, Paul and Silas
had hurried to Lydia's home. They were sure people would
be gathered there praying for them. It was wonderful for all
the new followers of Jesus to hear about such an amazing
miracle so soon after they had come to believe in him.

Lydia was getting closer to the river now and she slowed
down her walking so that she wouldn't have to cut short
her memories. Paul and his friends had left Philippi soon
after their release from jail. Lydia had often thought that
it was a shame that they couldn't have stayed just a little
bit longer. She would have liked them to have seen people's
faces when the tough jailer and all his family turned up
to their first meeting with the new believers in her house.
Paul had taught them that everyone was welcome to follow
Jesus. It didn't matter if they were rich or poor, old or
young—and Lydia soon found out how true that was. Her

home became a meeting place for the church in Philippi, and everyone was welcome there.

Lydia walked round the corner and saw the rocks where it had all begun. There was no one else there yet, and she went over and sat on the stone where she had first listened to Paul. She couldn't wait for him to arrive. She was sure he would come down to the river, to the place of prayer, as soon as he arrived in Philippi. It would be good to see him again. The church had grown so much since those early days. She had been the very first follower of Jesus in the city, but the church had grown quickly and they were all looking forward to meeting Paul. Lydia tilted her head backwards, allowing the warm sun to light up her face. She was so glad she had listened to what Paul had said on their first meeting. After all, it had changed her life!

The Bible tells us that Paul visited Philippi on other occasions and it seems likely that he stayed in Lydia's home. Lydia isn't mentioned again in the Bible, even though she was the first person to become a Christian in Philippi. Even when Paul wrote a letter to the church in Philippi, which originally met in Lydia's house, he didn't mention her by name. Lydia is one of the Bible's hidden heroes. As soon as she realized that what Paul told her was true, she brought her family and her servants to hear the truth about Jesus. And as soon as she became a Christian, she opened up her home to others, either for them to stay in or to use as a meeting place. Lydia had an open heart. She wanted to do what God wanted her to do, and she wanted to help other people. She is a great example to us.

What do you think?

1. Look at Acts 16:34. Why were all the jailer's family filled with joy?

2. Think! Paul and all his friends went down to the river to find somewhere quiet to pray and worship God. Do you ever find somewhere quiet where you can pray?

3. How did Paul feel about the church in Philippi every time he thought about them? See Philippians 1:3–5 for some help.

Home-sharers

The story of
Priscilla and Aquila

9

*(This story is based on
Acts chapter 18; Romans 16:3–5;
1 Corinthians 16:19; and 2 Timothy 4:19.)*

*P*riscilla huddled close to her husband, Aquila, as they watched the land slowly disappear from sight. She could remember so clearly the first time they had seen the coastline of Greece. Many years had passed since then, but the emotions she was now feeling brought all the memories flooding back. Aquila gently squeezed her arm. He understood how she felt; after all, they had been married for a long time and had gone through so much together. The journey back to Rome would take them many days. Hopefully the weather would stay calm and they wouldn't be too sea-sick!

'It feels strange to be going home,' Priscilla sighed, raising her voice so that she could be heard above the splashing of the waves. 'So much will have changed.'

Aquila nodded. 'At least Emperor Claudius has died and at last the Jews are allowed back into Rome,' he replied, a note of sadness in his voice. 'We've been banished from there for long enough.'

'It was all in God's plan, though,' smiled Priscilla. 'If Claudius had not forced all the Jews to leave Rome, we would never have met Paul and our lives would have been very different. Anyway, let's go down into the cabin; there's not much to see out here except water!'

Once on his bunk it didn't take long for Aquila's breathing to change into a gentle snore. Priscilla smiled down at him. He had been a good husband. Unlike so many men, he had let her help him in all aspects of his work, sometimes letting her take the lead with the things she could do better than him. She loved him dearly for allowing her to live a full and wonderful life; they had had so many adventures together. Priscilla's mind drifted back to their arrival in Corinth ...

They had heard that Corinth was a thriving modern city. It had once been destroyed by the Roman army but, since Julius Caesar had ordered that it be rebuilt, many people of different nationalities had moved there and seemed to live in peace together. As soon as they arrived in the city Aquila had gone to look for work and found a small house and a workshop where they had set up their tent-making business. It wasn't a usual job for a lady, but Priscilla had been willing to learn and was a hard worker.

They were both kept very busy in the workshop and they were glad when, one day, a man appeared asking for work. They had liked him immediately and had quickly given him a job. That was the start of a wonderful friendship. Paul had worked for them for eighteen months and they had learnt so much from him. He too had trained as a tent-maker, but it was the stories he told them about Jesus that Priscilla remembered most. After a while Paul had felt that both Priscilla and Aquila knew enough about Jesus to join him in teaching other people in the city. The three of them had so much in common and, when Paul decided it was time to move to another town, it had been an easy decision for Priscilla and Aquila to go with him.

Lying on her bunk Priscilla tried hard to smother a laugh as she thought about their journey to the port.

The boat was due to leave from Cenchrea, Corinth's eastern port. They had arrived early and Paul had suddenly announced that he was going to keep a promise he had made. Priscilla would never forget how different he looked when he walked out of the barber's shop with all his hair shaved off!

It had taken about ten days to travel to Ephesus. Paul had only stayed there for a short time before moving on to another place, but Priscilla and Aquila had decided to make Ephesus their home for a while. Before long, their house had become an important meeting place for the church. Everyone was welcome there. Priscilla and Aquila were always willing to share their home and their love for Jesus. It was a visitor called Apollos whom Priscilla remembered most clearly. They had first met him in the local synagogue and were impressed with the way he explained things about God. It had been obvious, however, that Apollos had never been fortunate enough to have someone like Paul as a teacher and there were many things about Jesus that he had never heard. Aquila and Priscilla had invited him into their home and spent many hours talking with him, explaining all the things that they had learnt from their friend Paul.

Back in the cabin it was beginning to get dark, but Priscilla smiled into the darkness. All the hours they had spent with Apollos had been worth it. He had moved to Corinth from Ephesus and, because of his teaching, many people had begun to follow Jesus. He was even considered nearly as important as Paul and Peter by many of the church in that city! It was good to hear from him from time to time. They still had many friends in Corinth. They would occasionally keep in touch; whenever Paul wrote a letter to the Corinthian church they would always send their greetings.

Priscilla could feel tears welling up in her eyes. She would miss Ephesus and the people they had left behind. There had been so many happy times in the city. She

had loved nothing better than for their house to be full
of people. She hoped that the church would continue to
grow without them; she felt sure that it would. But it
was time for a change and there was a new man leading
the church in Ephesus now. Paul thought highly of him,
and Timothy seemed to have fitted in well, despite being
very young!

'It wasn't all happy, though,' Priscilla whispered
out loud.

She gazed once more at Aquila still sleeping peacefully
beside her. She was glad he was there. It could so easily
have been a different story. For a moment, Priscilla
allowed her mind to wander to the bad times. They had
often been in danger. Many people in Ephesus didn't want
anyone to become a Christian and they spread horrible
rumours and caused riots, in the hope that they could stop
the church from growing. Priscilla winced as she thought
of the occasions when she and Aquila had even risked
their lives to keep Paul and other Christians safe. She
shook her head.

'Better to remember the good times,' she said to herself
firmly. 'Remember the good, but never forget how God kept
us safe in the bad.'

Aquila stirred in his sleep and opened his eyes. 'You
talking to yourself, love?' he asked sleepily.

Priscilla nodded. 'Just reminding myself how good God
has been to us,' she said, climbing out of bed. 'Let's go and
get something to eat.'

Priscilla and Aquila eventually arrived back in Rome. Paul sent them a special greeting when he wrote a letter to the Roman church. In it he thanked Priscilla and Aquila for saving his life and made it clear that there were many churches spread over a wide area that would always be grateful to them for all they had done. When Paul wrote, he also made it clear that there was now a church meeting in Priscilla and Aquila's house in Rome. So they continued to welcome people for many years to come. Not many people have heard about Priscilla and Aquila. They are two of the Bible's hidden heroes. They did not become rich or famous; they simply opened up their home so that people could learn about Jesus. They helped people whenever they could and, because of this, they had an enormous effect on people's lives.

What do you think?

1. Paul travelled long distances telling thousands of people about God. Priscilla and Aquila made tents and invited people round to their home. Who do you think had the most important job?

2. Have a look at 1 Corinthians 12:18 and 27. What does this tell us about what God thinks of the different jobs people do?

3. Is there someone who makes you especially welcome in his or her home? Maybe you could say thank you to that person!

Story-telling
The story of Luke

10

*(This story is based on
Luke chapters 1–3; Acts 1:1–2, chapter 16,
and chapters 20–28; Colossians 4:14;
Philemon verses 23–24; and 2 Timothy 4:6–11.)*

Paul walked quietly into the cabin and smiled when he saw what his friend Luke was doing.

'You writing again?' he asked, glancing at the parchment spread out on the table.

'There's a lot to write,' laughed Luke. 'You've certainly had a busy few days!'

Paul moved forward and peered over Luke's shoulder.

'Have you put down all about my trial with Festus and King Agrippa?' he asked.

'Yes, I have,' said Luke with a nod. 'It's interesting reading, but I still think the best part of the story so far is two years ago when you had an escort of 200 Roman soldiers, 70 horsemen and 200 spearmen when you were sent to see Felix.'

'Anyone would think I was dangerous,' Paul chuckled to himself.

'They don't seem to be too scared of you on this boat,' answered Luke. 'Julius, the centurion, seems to let you do whatever you want. You were the only prisoner who was allowed to get off the boat at our last port to visit friends!'

Paul shrugged his shoulders and pulled a face. 'He might have changed his mind about me by the time we reach Rome,' he muttered. 'After we've had weeks and weeks crammed together at sea.'

He paused and began to move towards the door. 'And every little detail will be recorded in your book,' he added.

As the door clicked shut, Luke slouched back in his chair. Paul was right; every detail would be recorded, just as it had been in the past. This time, though, it would be easier. This time he was travelling with Paul and would see at first hand everything that happened. That would add a different edge to the story. So many of his stories before had been put together after talking to people who knew Jesus or who later knew the disciples or Paul. He might never have met Jesus himself, but he had had some great interviews!

He remembered the time he talked to Mary, Jesus's mother. What a privilege that had been! She told him so many things, all the little details about his birth, things that nobody else knew. It had been such a shock for her when the angel Gabriel had appeared, but she had soon realized that she was an amazing part of God's plan for the world. He remembered how she repeated the song she had sung when she was pregnant with Jesus and visited Elizabeth. In his mind he could see her face as she described the shepherds' visit on the night Jesus was born; he could almost hear her voice saying, 'I treasured everything up in my heart' as she described Jesus as a young boy at the temple. She hadn't understood everything back then, but she trusted God totally to carry out the plan he had for her and the rest of the family. It had been good to talk to her. Somehow, talking to people who knew and loved Jesus added the personal touch to his writing. Luke smiled to himself; he was a doctor, but he also loved history. He liked nothing better than to record exact times and details of events, but his writing would be dull if it didn't include everyday stories about people.

Luke sighed as he thought about Jesus. After all his investigations he knew so much about him, but he would have loved to meet him. 'Oh well,' he said quietly. 'At least I know Paul.'

He flicked back through the pages of his book. He had first met Paul in Troas. Paul had been travelling with Timothy and some other friends and Luke had been fascinated to actually meet the man he had heard so much about. Soon after Paul had arrived he announced that God had told him they must go to a place called Philippi and Luke decided to join them on their journey. It had been an eventful trip. It hadn't taken Paul and his friend Silas long to get into trouble. Within days of arriving in Philippi they were beaten and thrown into prison! Luke had seen it all happen and had waited with friends at the house of a lady called Lydia, who had just begun to follow Jesus. Luke had wished he could go into prison and help clean his friends' wounds, but he wasn't allowed. There was nothing anyone could do but pray, and that is what they did. Prayed, until there was a knock on the door and Paul and Silas walked in! God had sent an earthquake in the middle of the night; the jailer had become a follower of Jesus; the soldiers that had beaten them had apologized; and the two men were free!

'Just another ordinary day in the life of Paul,' chortled Luke, turning to another page. 'He's certainly had an eventful life ...'

He smiled as he glanced down at the next story. '... Although some people would say that sometimes he talked too much!'

It had been a few years since Paul and Silas's time in prison. Luke had stayed in Philippi but Paul had carried on his journey, visiting many places to tell them about Jesus, before returning to meet up with Luke again. Together they had travelled back to Troas where they

spent the week. It had been the day before they were due
to leave that Paul had decided to give a farewell speech to
the church. Many people crammed together in an upstairs
room to hear what he had to say. At first, everyone was
fascinated, listening intently to every word, but Paul went
on and on and on! It was hot and stuffy in the room, and in
the lamp-light Luke could see that people were beginning
to drift off. Paul didn't seem to notice and continued to
talk. There was a young man called Eutychus sitting on a
window-ledge by an open window at one side of the room.
He was struggling desperately to keep his eyes open, and
his head kept jolting forwards until suddenly there was
a loud scream and Eutychus disappeared. He had fallen
asleep and fallen out of the window! Being a doctor, Luke
had rushed to help him, but the fall had killed him. As
people began to cry Paul rushed downstairs, threw his arms
around Eutychus and brought him back to life!

Luke sighed. He loved these types of stories. In the
first book that he had written he had recorded lots of the
amazing things that Jesus had done. The book he was now
writing was his second, and it contained loads of evidence
that Jesus's return to heaven hadn't been the end of God
doing wonderful miracles on earth.

From Troas, Luke had set off with Paul to make the
journey to Jerusalem. All his friends had begged Paul not
to go there. The authorities in Jerusalem were looking for
an excuse to get rid of him and it seemed silly to visit the
city, but Paul was sure that it was what God wanted him
to do. They had stopped on the way at the port of Miletus,
where some of the church leaders from Ephesus met them.
Luke felt a lump in his throat as he remembered their

sad faces when Paul explained that he would probably
never see any of them again. It had been so hard to tear
themselves away from them and climb back aboard the
ship. They had visited many other people on their way to
Jerusalem. Paul had made so many friends during his years
of travelling.

Luke shook his head. He had found it such a privilege
to meet all those people; now he knew personally many of
the names that would be recorded in his book. However,
things had happened in Jerusalem just as they feared
they would.

They had been warmly welcomed by the disciples there.
Paul had gone up to the temple and enjoyed seven days
catching up with old friends. It was on the seventh day that
some Jewish people began to stir up trouble and Paul was
arrested. From then on, Paul was passed from person to
person, from place to place. No one could decide what to do
with him. Luke visited him often. Paul didn't let himself
become miserable; he was convinced that God had placed
him in prison so that he could have the chance to speak to
all the important people in the land about Jesus. One day,
Paul had described how God had told him that he would
be taken to Rome, where he must continue to tell people
about Jesus.

Luke sat back and laughed quietly. Paul had been right
again! After two years in Caesarea they were now on their
way to Rome. There was no way Luke would let him travel
alone. He wanted to be there as a friend and as a doctor,
but also to find out more of Paul's adventures to record
in his book. When complete, he would send it to his friend
Theophilus. Theophilus had enjoyed the first story, but he

was keen to find out what happened after Jesus returned
to heaven.

Luke put down his pen. It was growing dark outside and
he wanted some fresh air. He stood up and walked over to
the door. He would go and look for Paul. Hopefully they
would eat a meal together and then sit gazing at the stars
while Paul told him more about his life. Then tomorrow
Luke would write it all down, and who knew who might
read the book in years to come!

Luke and Paul had an eventful trip to Rome. On the way
they were shipwrecked and Paul was bitten by a poisonous
snake. Once in Rome, Paul was allowed to live in his own
house with a solider to guard him. From there, he spoke
to many people about Jesus, just as God had promised. He
wasn't allowed to leave the house, but hundreds of people
came to visit him, and he spent time writing letters to the
churches in all the areas he had visited. Many of these
letters are now in our New Testaments for us to read. Luke
eventually finished his second book, and both his books are
in our Bibles. The Gospel of Luke is the first book he wrote,
and the Acts of the Apostles the second. Luke is the only
non-Jewish writer to be included in the Bible.

Although many people read the books that Luke wrote,
he is not well known as a person. Luke is one of the Bible's
hidden heroes. He didn't push himself forward as being
important; in fact, he doesn't mention his own name in
either of his books. He simply used his gift for writing.
Luke never met Jesus but he worked hard to find out as

much as he could about him so that he could pass it on to other people. Without Luke's writing there would be many things that we would not know about the lives of Jesus and Paul. He probably had no idea that 2,000 years later, God would still be using the words that he had written to change people's lives! We need to follow Luke's example and use any gifts that God has given us ... who knows how the things we do now might be used by God in the future!

What do you think?

1. Have a look at Acts 28:3–6. What happened when Paul was bitten by the poisonous snake? How do you think Doctor Luke felt when he saw what had happened?

2. Looking at Acts 28:30, do you think Paul was sad that he was under house arrest in Rome?

3. If Luke never met Jesus, why was he a good person to write about Jesus's life? Read Luke 1:3.

Making a difference
The story of Barnabas

11

*(This story is based on
Acts 4:36–37; 9:26–30; 11:19–26;
13:1–5, 13; 15:36–41; and 2 Timothy 4:11.)*

Paul had been under house arrest in Rome for a long time. He was becoming an old man. His eyes were failing, and now he could hardly read the letters which his scribe wrote down for him. There was little to do on the dark evenings when his friends had left and he was alone. He was glad he still had his memories. What a life he had led! Tonight, his thoughts turned to Barnabas. He had so much to thank him for. Without Barnabas, nothing would have been quite the same.

Barnabas had grown up on the island of Cyprus but he had moved to Jerusalem when Paul first met him. It was Paul's first visit to Jerusalem since he had become a Christian. He had been worried about what the other followers of Jesus would think about him. They all knew him as the man who had hated Christians, rounding them up to throw them in prison or have them killed. He had wondered how they would respond to him now.

And he had every reason to be concerned. The church in Jerusalem didn't want anything to do with him. He had hurt so many of their friends, and they were extremely suspicious that Paul was pretending to be a follower so that he could identify and arrest them. Paul had felt hurt, but he couldn't blame them. It was Barnabas who had gone to sort it out. He had called the Christians together and explained how Jesus had appeared to Paul and changed his life. He told them how Paul had had to be smuggled out of Damascus because he was telling so many people about Jesus that the authorities had got angry. Eventually, Paul was welcomed into the church, but, if

Barnabas hadn't been there, who could say what might have happened?

Paul turned down his lamp and climbed into bed. It would have been enough for Barnabas to have simply introduced him to the disciples, but a few years later he had given him a great honour.

By that time, Barnabas was one of the church leaders in Jerusalem and Paul had returned to his home-town of Tarsus. Then, one day, Paul had received a message that a man had come looking for him. He hurried to meet his unexpected visitor and found Barnabas waiting. Barnabas explained that he had been sent by the church in Jerusalem to a place called Antioch to spread the good news about Jesus. Because so many people had since become Christians he needed help teaching them, so he asked Paul to go and work with him. Paul had felt so privileged. Barnabas could have asked anyone to join him, and yet he had gone to find him, Paul! They had then spent a year together in Antioch. And what a year it had been! Hundreds of people had become followers of Jesus, and every day was full of teaching and meeting with the church. In fact, it was there in Antioch that the name 'Christian' was first used to describe Jesus's followers. Paul had learnt so much from Barnabas: the quiet way he got on with his work, and the way he encouraged all the people in the church to use any gifts they had. He never turned anyone away, never made anyone feel useless.

It was almost dark now in the prison house. Paul remembered his next journey with Barnabas. This time, they were not alone.

They had been sent out on a long journey by the church leaders. Everywhere they went, they were to tell people about Jesus. This time, Barnabas's cousin Mark was to go with them as their helper. He was a young man, and Barnabas had seen that there was something special about him. Paul wasn't so sure! Barnabas was always looking for ways to encourage the young people, but Paul would rather do the job himself. He didn't have much patience with people who would probably let him down. And he had been right! Mark had deserted them after only a short time and had returned home.

That was it as far as Paul was concerned. Mark had had his chance and had failed. He couldn't believe it when Barnabas suggested that they should take Mark with them again on their next trip! Paul hadn't realized then that Barnabas was doing for Mark exactly what he had quietly done for Paul when he searched him out to be his helper in Antioch. That was Barnabas's special gift. He didn't see what people were now—he saw what they could be, with just a little help! The argument which Paul and Barnabas had over Mark spoilt their friendship for a while. Paul joined up with Silas and went to Syria. Barnabas took Mark with him and returned to Cyprus.

In the darkness, Paul thought about the letter he had just sent to his good friend Timothy. He could remember almost exactly the words his scribe had written down: 'Get Mark and bring him with you, because he is helpful to me in my ministry.'

Paul smiled. How Barnabas would laugh if he read that! He had been right about Mark, and Paul had been wrong!

It was getting late; Paul was beginning to doze off to sleep.

People flashed through his mind, faces he knew well, faces he hadn't seen for years. So many of them were connected with Barnabas in some way! Many of them had become Christians through Barnabas's teaching; many others were now teachers themselves, travelling all over the world telling others about Jesus. Most of them would not be doing that if Barnabas hadn't encouraged them to try new things, to have a go at something even if it went wrong! Things often did go wrong, but Barnabas was always there to encourage them and give them a second chance. That was how he got his nickname! When he first met the disciples, he was called Joseph, but the disciples preferred to call him Barnabas because it meant 'the son of encouragement'.

Paul turned over on his bed. It was good to remember Barnabas, but he needed to get some sleep. Barnabas, his dear friend. Yes, he might be going blind, but in his mind's eye he could still see clearly the person who had had such a great influence on his life!

We don't hear about Barnabas again in the book of Acts after the disagreement over Mark. Paul continued to travel from place to place, telling many people about Jesus. As he got older, he wrote letters to churches in the places he had visited. Some of those letters are included in the Bible. Many people think that the author of Mark's Gospel is the same Mark who is mentioned in this story. In fact, more than half the books in the New Testament part of the Bible were written by Paul or Mark! What a difference it would have made to all of us if Barnabas had not taken the time to encourage and teach them! Barnabas is one of the Bible's hidden heroes. He was willing to stay in the background, happily encouraging others to do jobs that he could have done himself. He was always willing to give people a second chance. When we are young, we can be so busy doing things that we don't stop and think about other people. This story teaches us the importance of putting other people before what we want to do and of always giving people a second chance if they make a mistake. It teaches us to encourage other people, and not to give up on our friends if they sometimes let us down.

What do you think?

1. What do you think would have happened to Paul if Barnabas hadn't introduced him to the Christians in Jerusalem?

2. What might have happened to Mark if Barnabas had not given him a second chance?

3. Can you think of anyone who has encouraged you? How did it make you feel?

4. Can you think of situations where you could encourage other people?

Slave or free?

The story of Onesimus

12

*(This story is based on
the book of Philemon.)*

Onesimus lay on his bed in the darkness. It was the middle of the night, but his mind was whirling and he couldn't sleep. He could hear the familiar night-time noises out in the streets; they were strangely comforting when you were alone in the dark. This could be his last night in the beautiful city of Rome. It could be his last night of freedom. Tomorrow, he would return to the place he thought he had left for ever.

How strange his life had been! How different he was now from when he left the town of Colosse all those months ago! How different he was to when he had first arrived in Rome …

The noise of the Colosse slave market rang in his memory. People shouting their prices, men haggling over the cost of a man's life. He hated it. The noise, the smell, the fact that human beings could be bought for only a few pennies. It was wrong, and yet there he was, his hands bound and his feet in chains, hoping that his new master would not be too cruel. He thought of his family. What would they be doing now? Were they slaves also, or had they escaped the horror that was facing him?

'Lift your head, boy!' A guard roughly pulled his hair back so that he could be examined. Onesimus looked up into a kind face.

'I'll take him!'

That was the deal done. Money was exchanged, and from then on he was someone else's property. He would spend the rest of his life as a slave.

Thankfully, his owner, Philemon, was a kind man. Onesimus knew of many slaves who were badly treated.

They would often meet together in the marketplaces when they went to buy food and talk about their masters. Some slaves were kept without food for days on end, others were beaten, and many lived in awful conditions. But Onesimus had nothing bad to say about Philemon. He was treated well, had plenty to eat, and his living quarters were comfortable. Even so, he was not happy. Questions raced around his mind. Why should he be a slave? Why could he not go out and explore the big wide world and enjoy a life of freedom?

Onesimus would often listen at the door when Philemon held meetings in his home. Many people attended those meetings. They were Christians who followed a man called Jesus. Onesimus would wait on them, bring them food and wash their feet. There were often visitors at these meetings, people who had travelled to other parts of the world to tell the stories about Jesus. Onesimus loved to hear these stories. Not that he was interested in Jesus; it was the tales of places far away that filled his imagination. Places where a slave could never go—unless ... A plan began to form in his mind.

It took Onesimus weeks to work out the details of his escape. At times, he felt guilty. Philemon had only ever been good to him. Even if he had had a different job as a free man, it was unlikely Onesimus's living conditions would have been much better. But it wasn't enough. He longed for freedom!

It was the middle of the night when he gathered together his small bundle of possessions and the money he had stolen from his master and sneaked out into the street. It would be impossible for him to hide for long in Colosse.

He needed to get as far away as possible. He had worked out the distances. If he walked by night and hid by day it wouldn't take him long to arrive at the port. Once on a ship to a far-away country, no one would be able to find him—he would be safe. Even if people on the boat recognized him as Philemon's slave, there would be little they could do until the boat reached its destination, and by then, at least Onesimus would have had the adventure of having been at sea.

He boarded the boat without difficulty. The sailors were only interested in receiving the ticket money—they didn't mind who was on-board! He huddled down in a corner, hoping he wouldn't be seen. Other people arrived. No one seemed interested in a man curled up asleep.

Then he heard it! The noise of the anchor being lifted. Men shouting on the bank as they untied the ropes. Slowly, the boat began to move.

Onesimus peeped over the side at the water swirling beneath him. At last, he was free! Inside, he wanted to sing and dance; instead, he gazed at the land quickly disappearing into the distance and wondered what Philemon would do when he woke in the morning to find him gone. He jingled the stolen money in his pocket and pushed away the pang of guilt. It was going to be a long journey.

After many days, Onesimus arrived in Rome. The first sight of it left him speechless. The city was a vast network of narrow, winding streets with ornately decorated buildings dotted here and there. There was so much to see! His first few days were filled with wonder at all the new things to

take in and enjoy. He just wished he could get rid of the
niggling thought at the back of his mind. Wherever he was
and whatever he did, the face of Philemon would appear
and the guilt would return.

Then, one day, a strange thing happened. He was sitting
near a fountain in the centre of Rome when he overheard
some men talking. He wouldn't have taken any notice
except that certain words sounded familiar to him.

'Paul ... prison ... house arrest ... Jesus!'

That was it! Surely the men were discussing Paul, the
great leader of the church. The man who had once hated
Christians but whose life had been dramatically changed.
Onesimus had heard so much about Paul in Philemon's
home. Philemon himself had become a follower of Jesus
because of Paul's teaching! Often in the meetings, the
Christians prayed for Paul to be released from prison
in Rome so that he could come to stay in Colosse and
teach them.

Onesimus wondered if these men were going to see Paul
now. He couldn't resist following them as they began to
move down the street. The men stopped outside a small
house with two guards standing in the doorway. One man
went inside but came out shortly after. Onesimus waited.
Would he be allowed in? Should he speak to Paul? He
would love to see what he looked like, and there was no
reason to mention Philemon. He walked boldly forwards.

'I've come to see Paul,' he announced to the guards as
confidently as he could.

The guards stood back to allow him through.

Paul was sitting at a table, his scribe beside him. He
looked up at Onesimus and smiled. He seemed much older

than Onesimus had imagined, and it was obvious that his eyes were failing him.

'Can I help you?' Paul asked. 'I don't believe we've met before.'

Onesimus didn't know what to say. 'I just wanted to meet you,' he stuttered. 'I've heard a lot about you.'

'Are you a believer in Jesus as I am?' asked Paul. Onesimus shook his head. 'Not really,' he said. 'But I know a lot of people who are.'

Even at that first meeting they had talked for an hour. There was something about Paul that made you want to listen. He was only in prison for believing in Jesus, and yet he never complained. It struck Onesimus that Paul was in chains just as he himself had been as a slave, and yet Paul accepted his position and was making a difference to people's lives even like that.

Soon, Paul and Onesimus had become firm friends. Onesimus would look after him, bringing him clothes and food. Day after day, Paul would explain more about Jesus, until one day, Onesimus realized that he too believed what Paul was saying. Suddenly, it was all clear! Onesimus got down on his knees and asked God to forgive him and to change his life just as he had done for Paul.

There was one problem. Try as he might, Onesimus couldn't forget about Philemon. He knew that God had forgiven him, but he also knew that he needed to go and ask Philemon for his forgiveness. He had stolen from him and deserted him. He knew that there might be serious consequences if he returned to Colosse, but he also knew that he had to go. He was now a follower of Jesus, like Philemon, and he needed to go and sort things out.

It was with great sadness that he explained his feelings to Paul. He was surprised at the reaction he got.

'You must go,' Paul told him without hesitation. 'But you won't go empty-handed. I'll write a letter to Philemon telling him that you are a changed man. And, Onesimus, I'll give you the money to pay back what you stole from him.'

Dawn was beginning to break over Rome. Onesimus moved to the window to watch it for the last time in this city. In his hand, he held the letter Paul had written. Paul had made it clear to Philemon that he would love Onesimus to return to Rome to care for him while he was in prison. He had pointed out that, now Onesimus also followed Jesus, he should be more like a brother to Philemon than a slave. Now it was up to Philemon. Slave or brother, Onesimus felt at peace. Maybe he would spend the rest of his life as a slave, but at least he would know he was forgiven by God and had put right the wrong he had done.

We don't know what happened to Onesimus when he returned to Colosse. It seems likely that Philemon forgave him and allowed him to return to Rome to look after Paul during his time in prison, but we will never know for certain. What we do know is that Onesimus is a great example to us of someone whose life was changed by God and who tried to put things right with the people he had wronged. He is a hidden hero of the Bible. It might have

cost him a great deal to return to Colosse, but he trusted
God to go with him and to give him the strength to cope
with whatever happened. Sometimes there are things in
our lives that we need to put right. We may know that God
has forgiven us, but maybe we, like Onesimus, need to say
sorry to other people.

What do you think?

1. How do you think Onesimus felt as he arrived back in
    Colosse and prepared to meet Philemon again?

2. Why was it important for Onesimus to return?

3. Bible teachers think that Paul sent another letter with
    Onesimus when he returned to Colosse, the letter to
    the Colossians found in our Bibles today. Have a look
    at Colossians 4:7–9 to see if Onesimus travelled on his
    own when he returned to Philemon.

4. What do you think Philemon should have done when
    Onesimus returned?

About Day One:

Day One's threefold commitment:

~ To be faithful to the Bible, God's inerrant, infallible Word;

~ To be relevant to our modern generation;

~ To be excellent in our publication standards.

I continue to be thankful for the publications of Day One. They are biblical; they have sound theology; and they are relative to the issues at hand. The material is condensed and manageable while, at the same time, being complete—a challenging balance to find. We are happy in our ministry to make use of these excellent publications.

JOHN MACARTHUR, PASTOR-TEACHER,
GRACE COMMUNITY CHURCH, CALIFORNIA

It is a great encouragement to see Day One making such excellent progress. Their publications are always biblical, accessible and attractively produced, with no compromise on quality. Long may their progress continue and increase!

JOHN BLANCHARD, AUTHOR, EVANGELIST AND APOLOGIST

Visit our website for more information and to request a free catalogue of our books.

In the UK: www.dayone.co.uk

In North America: www.dayonebookstore.com

Twelve Hidden Heroes – Old Testament

REBECCA PARKINSON

94PP, PAPERBACK

978-1-84625-210-5

Many people dream of becoming rich and famous. We're fascinated by the people who seem important, but often we don't notice those who are working behind the scenes. The Old Testament is full of mighty heroes who won battles or did amazing things, but there are also many 'hidden heroes'. These men, women, boys and girls were willing to stay unnoticed in the background, but their lives made a huge impact on those around them. Here Rebecca Parkinson tells the stories of twelve people in the Old Testament who may not be well known but who were just as important as those in the spotlight. This is a companion book to *Twelve Hidden Heroes: New Testament*.

Rebecca Parkinson lives in Lancashire with her husband, Ted, and their two children. She became a Christian after realizing that the Bible isn't a boring old book, but a living book that is full of exciting stories that still change people's lives. A teacher and the leader of the youth work in her church, she now loves to pass the Bible stories on to others in a way that everyone can understand.

REBECCA PARKINSON

12
Hidden
Heroes

Bible people
who did BRAVE
THINGS for God

OT

DayOne